SACRED
NOTES

By

Mone Parker

Dedication

I would like to give thanks to all the people who read my thoughts and took time to allow my words to penetrate their soul. This too shall pass. Thank God.

Table of Contents

God Save Me from Myself

...through the wounds of my infliction, cutting deep.

...when I can't find my way from me, back to You.

...when my brokenness has me bound.

God save me from myself, God save me from myself.

Redefine my self-worth.

Testimony

My testimony will tell a life-story of survival. Some would say of the fittest. Mine, I tell you, tells a different story of healing and perseverance. I'm not sure where to begin because there is no end. Now where do I start? I came to a life that I know. Grew with people I wanted to know. Felt pushed aside. Felt no love. I began to search to feel it, even though it was said. It seemed to roll off the lips, ending in lies. Along came some others who needed the love I hadn't received. I did my best. Every individual has their own mind. Here we go. I began to feel feelings, didn't like them a lot. So, I turned to things to numb the spots that touched the pain. Wow. That road was bumpy but took me places. Too many faces. Just a disaster. Things turned nasty. Time passed me; it was a mess. I made a decision to make some provisions. It was the right decision. Things got better. I no longer had to fight. Along this journey I lost some things, not material. He was my firstborn grandson. I tell you this – my heart and soul were hurt. This can't be right. The deal breaker came when I made a mistake, didn't think. Thank God it could have been worse. My testimony begins, remember, I told you there is no end.

Treading Water

I can't even swim!

So, I realized I've been *treading water* all my life. From the womb to earth. Let me help you understand why my feet seemed out of the water. I thought by chance, by the bad things that happened, I was sinking fast. Bad decisions, making provisions, love thought found. Paid the cost of living lies. I can't really explain it. I changed my thinking patterns. I felt free, like I had wings. Now through my decisions, I'm much better off. I'm no longer sinking.

I'm *treading water*.

Where the Battle Took Place

It took place in a time. Demons, bad decisions, played my mind. A battle was brewing. Check this out. I didn't even know it. It was a feeling no pain putting drugs in my system. I was looking for love in all the wrong places. I was being lied to by someone I knew. Strange thing about it, I never knew who. Things started changing. I did some rearranging on the thoughts that filled my head. It became astonishing to me when my mind was clearer that was *where the battle took place*.

 Mistakes

I've made many *mistakes* by feelings wrapped-up in lies.

Mistakes continually ordered the thrill of the rides taken many places I didn't wanna go. I thought to myself, "this time I know better than to listen to the thoughts in my mind." I can't live in the past, that would be the *mistake* that shows I knew better. What I can tell you is now I'm much better because of the *mistakes* that made my past.

Death

Death came upon me by the spirits that flooded my mind. So much confusion from an illusion that the world laid for me, just a trap. It's amazing how *death* came at a cost without a funeral when my mind was closed. My body was cold. I had no feelings. Not a beat to my heart. It's strange how you know this is not life, something just don't feel right. To come back from *death* the spirit must be free.

Ask me how I know? I'm still breathing.

Courage

I built *courage* to stand through my hurt and pain through the lies I bought. My *courage* survived amidst the darkness that surrounded my mind. Many nights I lay drowning in what was supposed to be my life. Don't get me wrong. I played the part. Felt like a victim. Blamed the system. Blamed the men. Was I supposed to look at me? Somewhere down inside I knew that I would survive. So I took responsibility for the things that happened. Let go of the blame and the shame. *Courage* to stand, is how I became the future of my destiny.

Look What You Done

Look what you done! You done made a mess! By using your own mind, thoughts became wrong. Feeling numb almost lost your life to a senseless thing made of anger and doubt that clouded your judgement. You didn't get it. Couldn't find it. Searched for it. Now what? Do you think it was all for nothing? There was a purpose behind the situations that found you looking in a mirror at you. Before you could move on, to not turn back, you had to really look at *what you done*.

Sit Down and Let Me Talk

Sit down, let me talk. I need you to listen to the words I speak; the things that you never asked me. I made up in mind, I can't waste no more time. I need to express myself. Do you want to know my dreams, my hopes, and aspirations? Might sound silly. Do you know my favorite color? That was frivolous, this talk is serious; it just might take a while. We had some talks, for the most part, you might have thought that pacified. The part you bought of what we had as a relationship. See my mistake was to have you think, along with other things, that I was satisfied. The time has come, since you seem to have become so comfortable, that you realize I made up my mind to have you *sit down*, just listen, *let me talk.*

Bound

I been places, seen many faces, turned my life around. Let me help you see the places, for me, that eventually set me free. *Bound* by hurt; hurt by love; given much received less. The places that turned me around are the places where I thought brought me peace. I checked myself by looking at time; changed the faces and places that changed my life for the better. I'm no longer *bound.*

In Spite of Me

You call me your Queen.

You hit me *in spite of me.*

I prepare a home for you; with dinner prepared.

You show no gratitude.

I give, you take. All I think of me, is you. *In spite of me.*

My brokenness I hide until…

That one day was the last, you left to return.

In spite of me! The Queen was gone.

Do You Love Me for Who I Am?

The words flowed from your lips, like words to that song.

I Love you! You say nothing is wrong.

I learn to do, what is done by a title I do not hold.

Touches turn cold, I don't see your face.

I lie down and wait, for a time, that seems almost forgotten.

Do you love me? *Do you love me for who I am?*

No Bushes

No more hiding. I'm made bold. I'm beautiful.

No more lying, I'm truth made through my journey told.

No doubting. I'm the daughter of the King.

To know that I am loved, my birth released my destiny.

No bushes to stand to hide me.

I'm victorious and set free.

Seasons

Did you wonder of the *seasons* that your journeys had been through? The <u>winters</u> body held you. Then <u>spring</u> came raining down. The <u>summer</u> nights left you hot and fall feel through to cool the spots. You ever wonder why seasons change? Ask yourself, how you let the *seasons* change you. Change how your *seasons* change the setting of your soul.

Woman to be Covered

I am a *woman to be covered,* I deserve to be loved. I don't need you to beat me by your selfish hands. A *woman to be covered.* I am your Queen, not your rug to be stepped on. I am a *woman to be covered.* Through me your existence remains strong. A *woman to be covered.* From you is how I became. I am a *woman to be covered.* When they're gone, you're left to blame. A *woman to be covered* is always a woman. Watch the covers I proclaim.

What I Forgot

I grew, thought I knew. I knew, then I forgot.

I looked never found, I found and got lost.

Abandoned.

I found something; it wasn't right.

Looked inside. Beautifully I found me. She was love. She was kind. Me. The victorious woman.

Now I know *what I forgot*!

In Spite of Broken Pieces

I rise from the dirt you throw.

You see pain, sometimes you don't,

Of a journey, meant to tear down my soul.

In spite of broken pieces, you show me how to grow.

I'm the force of birthing seeds.

Broken pieces you left are no longer broke.

My new journey, started with rebuilding the broken pieces of my soul.

Through Frightened Eyes

Through frightened eyes you showed things that couldn't be love. Frightened eyes a misconception of how to be loved. Eyes tell the tale of bondage and defeat. *Frightened eyes* filled with tears of surrender. I closed these frightened eyes and got down on my knees. Then I rose from the floor, what a wonder these *frightened eyes* did see.

The Wall

Childhood memories, some lost, some remembered. *The wall* protects the young, thought he loved me. Now I see. Our baby cries and we are all alone. And even when I know it's wrong and let you back for a claim for a body not yours to own. Now I stand with *the wall* on the other side.

Intimidated by Intimacy

Intimidated by intimacy.

Closeness touched without love.

Intimacy taken away, forced to lay uncovered,

uncovered in blood.

Intimidated by words spoken, bound by a selfish being.

Intimated by intimacy you left my soul lost to intimacy.

I feel intimidated to share my intimacy freely.

Intimated by intimacy, no longer am I bound.

Broken Hearts of a Torn Family

Broken hearts of a torn family not my own.

Broken promises, some that were never told.

Broken pieces like a broken puzzle thrown.

Broken thoughts, through a torn family decision.

Broken hearts. Broken family mended from the *broken hearts of a torn family's* soul.

Woman, the Receiver

Created to receive. Through my body gives life. *Woman the receiver*, through my father, a King, made me right. Stand before you astonishment sees your eyes at the beauty laid before you, and the wonder of my deliverance, a creator made for you. *Woman the receiver* I bare the world Kings and Queens. *Woman the receiver*, maker of beautiful things.

Damaged Places of the Past

Damaged places hold victim to my soul. Lost visions of my desires and blur red dreams I hold. These *damaged places* gamble with the love I deserve. These *damaged places* fight the rhythm of my beating heart. Those *damaged places* that had me bound are *damaged places* of my past.

Injured

Injured are the journeys of my past. Some hidden. Some told. The bondage my mind keeps locked away sometimes I hold. I forsake me, my spirits are gone. Left alone, flashes of life lost are the stories left untold. The injuries no longer bind me. My spirit is set free. *Injured* is a journey. I stopped because of all the injuries. I'm finally free.

A Story

This is the beginning. A good story has an ending. The writer takes you through and helps you picture what if you were the one your eyes read through the lines. Could you begin to imagine by what your mind kept through the book? How could you have handled everything? Would you have played the game? Have you lost you? Found you? Hurt you? Betrayed you? Walked to breathe again? Found a love always there, that never left you? Been taken on a ride? Stripped to receive again through frightened eyes. Circumstances of thinking left consequences, holding places of needless tears of a soul at war with your body. Emptied fantasies can't stop remembered places of a working arrangement for an unfulfilled need. Thinking your body was made for man. Intimated by intimacy. Damaged places of your destiny. The door of life healed and released me, of what I forgot. In spite of me, I'm the daughter of a King.

Mad at Me

Would you be mad if I gave you something and looked at you as someone else? The feelings inside exploded with the thought of your touch, haven't had it in years. Not that I'm thirsty, or desire who you are. Just because feelings weren't there. I longed for a touch, passed what I saw. Closed my eyes to visualize a face, being the touch against my body. It wasn't a fantasy, what if, or just a one-time thing. My body was made for man alone. If you know what my body is made for, then you will discover; what you think you can do, can't equal to what my body is used to. So, upon discovery, it's only fair to let you know you could have been a one-time thing. Like man, I have to let you go. This is just a woman-to-woman talk. I hope you understand what I thought about on how to misbehave is just how it is. Now I'm talking woman to man. I'm the nature found in a grown ass woman. I did it to feel what I was used to getting. All-in-all, it's just the same. No blame. No excuse. Experience is the best teacher. You're excused. Class is over.

 Jigga

It was a year and a time I'll never forget. My heart shattered. My soul ached, yet I stood ready to fight. I must go back just a moment. It was October 11, 2003. I watched him come from the womb of my child. Amazed the life I saw with my heart filled with joy. It was like I gave birth with my Ja'lyon Jermene Johnson. I called him my *Jigga*. It had been two years since I had come home again. He became my sunshine. I watched him grow, walk, run, play, fall and talk. I was the only one who did his hair and he didn't cry. How can I explain September 26, 2009? When someone took his life. At work I got a call screaming in my ear…" MOM, JIGGA GOT SHOT!" I yelled. Left work. I arrived and she said he got shot in his chest. I fell. Then I knew he was gone from [this] life. Raced to find my daughter. When at the hospital, a calm came. Didn't understand then, now I know it was God preparing me for the suffering.

Who Are You?

I make no excuses for the choice I made. The decisions that led me down a path of self-destruction. It wasn't a pity party. It felt like an enjoyable time. I look back, not to analyze. It's a tape I play for myself. I walked in shoes, different sizes, different brands. Even as I walked, different people claimed the shame of things I done and the steps I took. I can try to explain what it feels like to look at someone doing something. It looks like you, yet you don't understand. Why they did what they did and is this happening? *Who are you?*

The End

Could I become what I may have fought? I got a yearning deep in my pit; bypass what you seen. Couldn't imagine this far. My demeanor had changed. Was it the attention? Curiosity? or things deeply hidden? Had enough of old habits. Could that be the excuse? Change the game, change the reason. You went too far. Watched by many, chosen by me. Wait…stop. I chose how this must end when it begun began.

Heart Of

Heart of blood and vessels made stone by life's cold lessons. Beating a slow rhythmic beat lay cold by things called love. Heart made true by the Divine, lay frozen in my chest. So heavy a burden to carry with my heart beating barely. *Heart of* life, heart of mine, was a heart felt left behind. *Heart of life*, heart so true, you deserve to be renewed. So my gift to you I bring is to chip away the ice and restore the beating to the *heart of* life.

Made Right

I don't claim to be the virgin Mary, Elizabeth or even Sarah. I did a lot of things. I had to bear my soul to bury. Fought demons that clouded my thinking. Fought my flesh, from tying my soul. Fought the world to take my place. Man can't stand alone. Fought daddies to care for his children. Yet, you know the most important fight is when I didn't fight no more and my Father forgave me and again I was *made right*.

Taken Hostage

I was *taken hostage* by faces I did not know. Taken on a ride, felt like twists and turns, quick stops, and some layovers. *Taken hostage*, the voice changed. I never seen a window. Eyes covered by pieces of life flashing like a strobe light. The voices began to slow down and talk to me real slow. I listened closely because I thought I heard someone I knew. When I finally said a word, my eyes would reveal I was actually in the mirror taken hostage by self.

Something I Missed

Things started happening at a very quick pace. Wasn't sure. Didn't know I had entered a race. Didn't realize time was ticking. I ran faster. I didn't want to lose because from the moment the clock started, I just knew I needed to be up front. I was going and going. It was like the race was never ending and I didn't look back. When I slowed down, I was shocked. My eyes looked at the clock. That's when I really realized that through the race there was *something I missed*.

You Wanted It

You came with a plan after your eyes did discover the things laid under my clothes. We flirted a while, made eyes at each other. You claim it was my smile. Timed passed by. I didn't make it easy. I had enough of all that. A couple of meals did the movie thing. The deal wasn't quite sealed. It wasn't long before my thoughts and emotions gave in to what my body was feeling. We didn't plan it to happen, yet it was bound to proceed, to things that people who like each other do. After it was over, my body wasn't right. My mind knew that's all *you wanted*.

Stripped to Be Redressed

Stripped of all that's worldly. Redressed to be born again. Stripped to redefine the phenomenal woman. Redressed with dignity and pride. Stripped and cleansed body and mind. Redressed to improve an unconscious state of being left far behind. Stripped down bare and naked my soul was bound to loose. Redressed to be redeemed and released at my Father's gate in Heaven.

Wounds of Suffering

Cut deep the *wounds of suffering*. My wounds I made by deceit. The lack of just because wasn't my fault. I carried the wounds even those of my mother and my father. I was taught whatever happens was a family thing. So, through my life those are the things I kept to myself. Confused, never corrected those lies that I bought; carried around on my back like a solder going to war. Now don't get me wrong. I learned right from wrong. Only to discover I became a creature of habit. As time went on, when I didn't belong or felt unloved, I covered my body with blankets. They made me feel warm wherever I was at. Just like onions, the blankets peeled away every lie I laid under. It wasn't a surprise when I discovered the *wounds of my suffering*.

 Fractured

Fractured, spoken, my soul was speaking. I couldn't deny it anymore. The thoughts through my mind, like mice running around a maze trying to get out. While the world just stood and watched. *Fractured*, not broken, there is still hope, for the child and the girl to become that dream she spoke.

Healed

Healed from the pain of my past mistakes. *Healed* from the bondage from too many heartaches. There's no denying when you think your grown, think you got your head on straight and you're wrong comes to bite your ass. Still you say "nothing's wrong". Different decision same mistake. I'm beginning to think could this be fate. Not realizing you never took the chance to see what caused your trouble. Step back. Change your decisions. Bow down. I realize I have been *healed*.

Soul Tied

Soul tied not even knowing when you lay down your body, the soul starts to float out. You become more than the soul you lay under. Moved aside by this new encounter, didn't realize your soul moved too. Had a party. Wasn't invited. It was more than your body could hold. Despite what you thought you never knew your soul was now *soul tied.*

You Played Yourself

You came like pimp daddy. I heard rumors about your style, your looks, your charm, your "debonair." All a façade. It was the women who allowed you to be what you are not. Yeah, I may have come along. You heard some things about me too. Don't judge a book by its cover. Things aren't always what they appear, the truth lies in the heart of me. So now go back to your research. *You played yourself.*

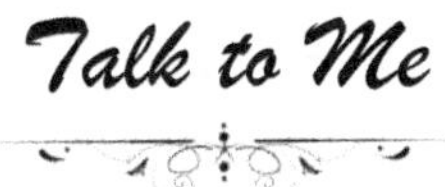

Talk to Me

We played play talk at first, like "what's up?" "Where's your man?" Those weren't really the things that were on your mind. You wanted much more. Couldn't help yourself. A lot of conversation was a waste of your time. I avoided the obvious. Your journey, your charm, became weak. You wanted to move fast that was your style. Haste makes waste. It was time, you felt, to go inside. I watched the demeanor. I began to feel sick because all you needed to do was *talk to me*.

Stories

I heard childhood *stories*. Some call them fairytales, you know when at the end of the story everything is well. Never wondered why in those stories hardly anybody cried. Now don't get me wrong, I know most of it wasn't real, but from my eyes it always seemed happy endings became real. No one ever told me that those *stories* were *stories* I was never in.

Time to Examine

Chances are we look for things, to try to fill a void: clothes, food sex…I could name more. We avoid the inner knowing that tells us quit feeding ourselves these lies. Through circumstances and situations at best, we try to cope. There's no rhyme or reason, no shit just happens. Why me, or ifs, ands, or buts. Take a look around and as you stop, you will blatantly see that everything that happened has set you up for a *time to examine* what you didn't examine in time.

Always in a Hurry

I got to go. Time's moving too slow. Seems like I'm moving in slow motion. Started going fast at a young age. How could I have known? Felt like life carried me much faster than some others. I developed fast, liked the boys. They liked my fat ass. Soon I'd discover it was just a downfall. Became a parent. Ran the streets. Thought I was having it all. Now I discovered what I thought I knew came from *always being in a hurry*.

First Love

First love led me around. I was like a child looking for a lost toy never found. *First love* had me wondering if love was always beneath those covers. But time passed. *First love* changed; I was beneath the blankets alone. Now through these changes the pillows were wet, the heart felt broke and alone. By myself in bed, I realized and said while the thought filled my head of being my *first love*, first.

Needless Tears

Needless tears, lay swallowed by weeping lips, telling a story of sorrow. Tried to wipe away all the pain left of empty promises. I couldn't catch my breath, my dreams I thought had left. Wasn't my fault, I did my best. I had to sit back and think, will my yesterday be my tomorrow? Took a while. I changed my direction. Those *needless tears* made my vision clearer.

Masturbation

Hmmm…I missed your touch. You left me. It became too much. I began to go to a place where only I could see your face. It started the way you used to…touching me slow. Caressing my body. Sometimes I felt your kisses. Every night we would meet at our secret place. Wait it gets deep. I'd pretend you would taste me then continue to penetrate me. It was everything you were. It even had your name. I called you several times, not like I used to call you daddy. Suddenly the feeling was gone. It was the end of my *masturbation*.

Holding Places

Fixed on an idea. Holding places of situations had started to become real. I held on to pain from a child. The memories moved down the right side. Held on to the lost love that placed itself beneath my heart. Held on to unwilling daddies. It was an ache in my gut. Held on to things I began to tell myself, it held a place inside my mind. Now I realize *holding places* for me *holds places* I no longer dwell.

 Watched

Emotions run through, the faces hiding the pain. Voids of discomfort, anger, loneliness, and bad decisions, show feelings the body claim. Phone calls… sometimes anger, sometime laughter and sometimes tears. Bodies cross to forbidden boundaries of empty lust, sometimes thought unseen. *Watched* as we are looked upon by someone unknown of our struggles. *Watched* the defensives, the character defeats of beautiful women caught in inner turmoil.

Healed and Released

Healed from the damage to fine some peace. *Healed* from stories never mentioned, pain just too deep. *Healed* to be free. *Released* from a world I let tear me apart. *Released* because my freedom was bodily bought. *Healed and released* from the womb to the grave.

Crippled Limitations

Crippled limitations torn down my self-worth through history or genetics of life, which was worse? *Crippled limitations* came from others struggles and inability to move beyond. *Crippled limitations* tried to play my history's song. STOP. I started standing and walking, gave my history a new song. *Crippled limitations* are now the strength to my calcium rich bones.

Chained to Circumstances

Legs chained down having no key. *Chained to circumstances* that altered me. People placed in my path. *Chained to circumstances*, thoughts and feelings that would not set me free. Running races that had no love story end. *Chained to circumstances* my legs finally broke free. My heart held the key.

Journeys

Where my *journey* began, my destiny stopped, deep in those lost, haunting memories. Where my mind lets me wonder and even lets me cherish thoughts dull and aching, I thought I had buried. Where my heart sometimes aches, and I have to touch me to feel the beat. Where my life would have been, could have been, should have been and has not been, yet. Is where my new *journey* begins, and my destiny awaits.

Each Day

Each day I face a decision; stay in yesterday or reach for tomorrow. *Each day* I face a person, the reflection says she's me. *Each day* I know tomorrow is another day began. *Each day* I know yesterday holds pieces of my past. *Each day* I remember, yet the memories fade away. *Each day* I am stronger. She has begun to make memories of not yesterday or tomorrow, just *each day.*

The Roadmap to Before

Just jumped in the car while the engine was running. I took the road; didn't see where it was going. Took me places I didn't want to go. I followed anyway. How did I know I was looking for something in me, wanting it through you? It was uphill, downhill, winding roads, speed bumps…a couple of crashes too. The trip is over. You stopped the ride. Now I'm on the *roadmap to before.*

Hurting Woman with a Past

There she is. You can't see her pain. The tears she finds in her own mirror of shame. Sheltered nor privileged, seldom told she was loved. She saw many things young. Suffered battles of abuse, told this is love. *You're a good little girl. This only between me and you.* Now her path to find love is made through what was used of her. *Hurting woman with a past* holds the hurt no more.

Door of Life

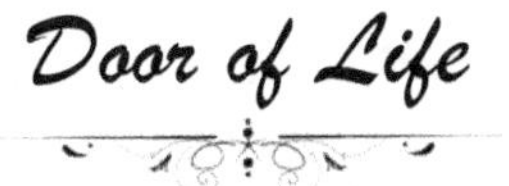

I opened the door, the wind knocked me down. Closing the door, the harder the sound. Opened the door the *seasons* changed. Closing the door, I met with blame. I opened the door, love lied. I became a mother. I tried closing the door. I was left standing alone. The *door of life* open, closes, even revolves sometimes. The *door of life* is open, leaving the past behind.

Impregnated by Destiny

The seen vision. Once dreamed by a child. Love sought by a
body on fire. Not the abuse required to show love by an empty
soul. I stood accused by inner demons, holding life in the palm
of my hands. Not by desire, yet by faith. I'm *pregnant by destiny*
when I reach heaven's gate.

My Character. My Fire.

My character defines my being.

Though sometimes out of place.

Some values I lost along the way.

I'm human. Yes, I make mistakes.

I'm forgiven. I did wrong.

My fight through adversity, my fire can't be put out.

It started in my mother's womb.

In To Me I Let You See

In to me I let you see, the hurt behind the face.

In to me I let you see, things I though you would erase.

In to me I let you see, the little girl who called you daddy.

In to me I let you see, the distance of my soul.

In to me I let you see, things of me, weak and destroyed.

In to me I let you see, I let you have it all.

Now in me, I let you see a woman passed the hurt.

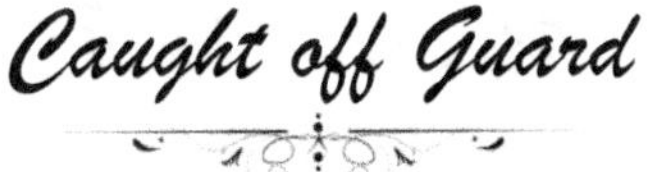

Caught off Guard

Caught off guard. Yes. I knew better. Cast aside by my own decisions, torn inside by emotions unfulfilling. Judged by myself. The harshest of critics unable to clear the remnants of blurred-eye vision. Mind tortured by those selfish decisions. Soon the uncomfortable dis-ease inside was comfortable and fulfilling. Thoughts of change can't undo already broken dreams. I tell you no lie. I felt content and in control of things. The rhythm of life seemed soothing and became my best friend. Doubts, mistakes, uncertainty, and regrets change me. I can no longer hide. I will reach who I need to become in the blink of an eye.

Woman Down

A woman born to a King; guaranteed a dream; promised eternity. A woman came from a rib, in a garden of everything. Bestowed with the greatest treasures. Life abundant that would last forever. Betrayed by the lack of God's will instilled in her thoughts. A woman guilt ridden takes away her piece of Heaven. A woman shamed and scared; hid the nakedness of her troubles. A woman never knew of the curse upon a nation. A woman never knew of the grace she would be forgiven. Now this woman knows the cross which Jesus paid for her.

Sat Down

I sit and remember better times in my life. Watching babies grow, dreams half-ass and a few talk shows. Bad decisions, everyone challenges self once in a while. I've been placed where decisions are made for me. Some good, bad, and indifferent. I want to take time to look over my life with some wonder of how I chose to be self-inflicted.

The Other Woman

Inside me lies the *other woman*, who claims my victory.

Patiently waiting, for the wonder that has been kept hidden.

She lies bound as a child lost by a broken past.

She grows searching through a looking glass, broken.

She finds no comfort in the love she seeks.

The *other woman* comforts to protect the investment given on my
Father's consignment of a guarantee lasting forever.

Defeat to Victory

My defeat played my mind. I stood frozen in time.

By a victory not won and a life not begun.

Defeat came with a cost, yet my battle wasn't lost.

Victory took some training and perseverance.

Defeat battled with honor, the title I wanted to keep.

Victory I finally won. I stand delighted in my stature.

My Father's Inheritance

I have a claim of victory, a purpose, and a life.

I have a claim of life never ending, no pain, loss, or strife.

I have claim to be reminded of what my heart felt.

I have a claim to sing of deliverance, sing of being set free.

I have a claim, no one can take. I'm His daughter from the womb, I have a claim on my *Father's inheritance.*

Tongue Against Me

Tongue against me, torturer of my soul. *Tongue against me,* talked about the dreams I had, the love I lost, things good and bad. My tongue spoke of falseness, to cloud already mangled thoughts. My tongue tasted demons and filled my body with poison. At last, my *tongue against me* spoke of a future I would have.

Desperate Spirit

Desperate spirit had me bound, by the evil that surrounded my mind. Brokenness, bitterness, abandoned and let down. *Desperate spirit* took away self-esteem, self-worth and pride. Laid my body with enemies, all those empty spirits blocked the shame and told me lies. *Desperate spirit* was left all filled up and broken down. *Desperate spirit* searched and found the living sacrifice that set me free.

I Thought

I thought I could tame and train you. Make you what I liked and what I needed. It was a "tedious job." I worked a lot of overtime. No pay increase at all. No different plans. No pretend one-night stands. No dinner dates. No private dances. I fed you. I loved you. I forgave you and fought me to keep you. The one thing that changed me became crystal clear. All this time *I thought* you loved me.

Never Told

I thought I had been told everything of the things I should have paid attention to. I changed the way everything should have been played because I thought I knew what fit me best. It became a mess. I played slip-n-slide, ring-around-the-rosy, hide-n-seek, plus a few others. Things seemed to get worse, there was nothing much to do but rethink my choices and do better. Now I can't say through all my mistakes and decisions that I was *never told.*

Confused Orgasms

This is a sit down. Something that needs your undivided attention. It starts in the mind, that embraces your body and slowly gets better with time. Everyone is different; big, small, or indifferent. Performed by humans, batteries your preference. Let's start slow. The mind talks to the body about a little party. You are the guest. The invitation speaks about a pleasurable time stating you are the guest of honor. The place is your bedroom. The cake is you. And oh what fun it will be unwrapping the presents! Invited are just a few guests. Did I say the party lasts as long as you want? Now don't be surprised if some guests arrive in their party suits too. Don't get this wrong. Celebrations lasts longs. It's my party and I do how I please. The party was over, the guests had gone. Each day I celebrated with a new gift. Take it how you please. I wasn't real bad, its' just I had a celebration of *confused orgasms*.

Escape Charges

I got *escape charges.* I ran from the captive of my soul. The body I laid next to had kept me prisoner for far too long. It was time to go. Let me tell you how he first caught me. It was looking for love. Had baby daddies. Had done things for far too long. I was feeling weak. My mind confused, playing a game of cat and mouse. I thought nothing could touch me. I had been through enough which made me strong by my so-called history. A lie told in mind. It was after the mystery man, I thought, came to my rescue that I was okay. To my surprise, he showed me more than I bargained for. He played how I like. He made tempos in my bed. Felt like I'd been chained down. Then something changed. He didn't play right. The tempo slowed down. He loosened the chains. I waited till he slept. I slipped loose and was gone. The funny thing about my escape charges that night is he never looked for the fugitive of the charges he kept. She was cleared and totally free.

He is My Friend

We didn't start out on the worst of terms. We called each other silly names, played games. Told each other so many things. Where you see him, there I was. We stuck like peanut butter and jelly. No one really knew how our relationship was. If we kissed or had sex, really wasn't their business. We never flirted, dated, or talked about being together. We had the best relationship ever. Theresa confession I need to make; after all that time I did want to kiss his lips because I had watched them move for many years. I'm glad it didn't happen because today he is still my friend.

I Changed My Mind

I changed my mind on so many things. It was like I was going in circles. My clothes, my cars and most of all, the color of my hair. I had changed my mind on different lovers. No particular reason, just because I thought I could. Why not? Changed my mind on the reasons of how I was feeling. Didn't want to waste my time. Then the biggest change in my mind happened. Really not a shock when I changed my mind, to change the times that my mind changed me. That had become a habit.

Emptied

Emptied out, given up. Too much had filled my soul. I had taken all I had just to fill a void. I was so empty, felt like I was walking on air, all those soul ties. What you think? All those souls seemed to carry me along for the ride. *Emptied.* Because I was shaken along, not filled by righteous things. Now I'm a single soul on a mission to fill the empty spots that lay vacant by souls I *emptied* out.

Fantasies

Fantasies grandiose, filled my mind of wants, spoken, seldom seen. These *fantasies* weren't of riding on white horses, just of deserved things. Like a man who really loves me, appreciates who I am. We both have a job, start a family and live happily ever after. Not that I lived in *fantasy* land, this *fantasy* was in my head. See the thing about *fantasies* that stay in your mind they turn into fake short stories, where you believe you are someone else.

Back Up

Back up, wait a minute; I done put too much of me in it. I done gave it all just because I had a feeling I was winning! I done made up my mind if I'm wasting my time. I've got to get it plus some! In it, this is how I run this shit!! Come when I call, play by the rules, your just a good *back up*.

Appointed Healings

I've had *appointed healings*. Like when the enemy had my soul poisoned and bound, death just behind the door. When I couldn't see, face swollen for a week from a beating, not by my father. When the pills didn't work, the knife wouldn't cut, the smell of gas too strong. Sometimes I felt like giving up. Done too much. Wasted too much time. I'm appointed for healings. My circumstances don't have a chance. I'm made for appointed purposes.

I Forgive Me for Me

I forgive me for me and all the things I kept blaming me for. Blame for the lost love. Blame for my misbehaving. Blame for destroyed souls, thinking I was saving them. I lost me for no good reason other than me thinking not of me first. *I forgive me for me*, that let hands beat me and identify it as love. I forgave me to find me passed the blame.

Transformed

I done did it. Done changed the game. Caught a glimpse of some forbidden shame. Done looked at something totally out of character. I be singing of some things just bad experiments gone wrong. Lonely calls from the emotions of something missing or haven't had that experience, yet. I learned something very quickly: behavior feelings forbidden can't be what my body learned while hidden. The feeling gotten by man can be replaced by not looking at gender.

Dead Issues

Dead issues play sequences of events that should have been dead and gone. A constant reminder. A mind changer of things that are done. The things that led to the issues, that had some consequences, that changed the state of my being. If letting sleeping things go was or is the answer, my mind is often reliving, playing funerals with my vision while I still face *dead issues*.

Who You Say I Am

I can't be labeled by what I've done. *Who you say I am* is an unspoken truth? Have you seen what I've seen? Felt what brought me tears? Have you had to go through degradation? Been a slave to a poison? Lost your soul and walked through fire to find you? *Who you say I am* can't bind me. Your thoughts can't fill my head. Your journey, I can't follow. Who I know I am leads me pass *who you say I am*. Your words have no truth.

I did somethings, rarely thought about who or why. Life seemed to be going not of dreams. So, I decided to take what I call life on a ride. Damn! What a rollercoaster. Ups, downs, circles…really no straight up and lots of bends. Eventually it came to a stop. My head was spinning. I felt a little sick. Had to sit down. Soon I'd discover after the motion of a rather long ride, I couldn't do that again. That was a scare. I made up in my mind that I had a *life of importance*.

Without You

I had thought you might have been made just for me with the illusion I brought, and eventually played on myself. You gave some things. I guess it was too much for me to think that always you would be my forever. Slowly you faded. You would return. I'd be content, didn't bother to question you. You were, for the most part, my escape. Things started dangling in my mind this last time. I couldn't shake it, so I closed my eyes, opened to the light that I'm much better for me, *without you.*

Not by My Past

Not by my past am I defined by what you may have heard or what you may have seen. You never looked through the eyes of a wounded child becoming a fractured woman? Yet I discovered who I'm not. My past. Pains never forgotten through scattered lies and, different people. A fractured woman found lessons worn by a fractured soul. *Not by my past.* Today I am set free. Fractured not broken. My life is made whole. *Not by my past.*

Scattered Lies

Scattered lies, like the flow of a stream running through my mind. Casting out my dreams. Telling me early on truths believed by a young mind. *Scattered lies* through most of my life. After some time, the scattered lies would mold from a fold uncovered a fractured soul left in a world designed to entrap, control and destroy. *Scattered* lies no longer sing lullaby's that soothe a young soul. My truths speak freedom from *scattered lies* of my past unfolded.

Different People

I'm *different people*. I realized I played some part of the role people I played in my life. The little girl scared and lonely. The young lady, her inner soul torn apart. The mother raising children alone. The woman who had enough. Her heart, her exterior tough to breakthrough. *Different people* still linger. Only now they are much stronger. I'm *different people*. Just holding this life challenged by life that *different people* built.

Wanting You

This shit has got me someplace feeling some way I don't like; didn't know I would, could or rather should, feel the way I do. Things to the world may look like they should not be. I can't blame it on lust, loneliness, or just because. I've been the type to see what I like and get it. Didn't know it would be like this. I don't want to pull away. It ain't familiar, just the same; I want it. Don't look at me like you know who I am. Everything you see was already planned. The purpose of my position fought in another's mind. What allows you to think because you think you see what I do, to assume you think what is best before you take a look at you. Yes. Our paths crossed, a short conversation or two. Told you what you needed to hear to soothe your clouded mind. Me, I'm not that important, at least not to you. Can't understand when you have no clue of the history that follows, that you see me daily and figure I might not be made for woman that I am.

Body Tamed

I was young, my body was right. It wasn't until my body was touched that I lost sight. How I behaved with my body was no excuse. I believed I had the right. I had given my body in spite of love, never forced to perform. I enjoyed what I did, my body led me. I was blindsided. I felt compelled to misbehave. I had become my own slave to instant, delayed, and self-satisfaction. For the most part, the position I gave was satisfying for me. I'm no longer confused. My *body tamed* by me I no longer use.

Soul Epidemic

I don't remember the sounds that I heard. It was enough for me to clearly hear and understand. I couldn't ignore it was a cry for help. The poison had control. Nothing was right. I could barely function. My body was leaving signs of distress, calling for relief. The liquor had done it; the weed took me high. Cocaine became crack and shattered my world. Yes. Today I am free. You don't know if I don't tell you, that I survived a *soul epidemic*.

Old Faithful

Old faithful did me right.

Old faithful was young.

We played this game for different reasons.

I didn't get or we didn't have a love connection.

Yet what we had was good to the last drop.

Look…I'm telling truth.

I might have wanted to be his, how *old faithful* put it down.

Yet now we played while *old faithful* was around.

Just wouldn't lead to anything else.

Old faithful was there about 2 ½ years.

Almost like I couldn't give him up.

Things happened.

What he had was beginning to run low on supply.

The game changed, yet he was still *old faithful.*

I still wanted him.

He was my high demand. He filled my sexual appetite.

Old faithful was there. I think he enjoyed it too.

I seen him this one day, years later.

My sexual appetite started stirring.

My body went back to what we used to do.

I really wanted to feel it again.

He was with someone.

So, I just said *"hello"* and kept my hunger hidden.

For My Freedom

I'm being true about the things that these lines unfold for your eyes. No half-ass from my soul experience. I share these things for my freedom. I used to write years ago, thought it was a waste of time. Busy moving. Life showing up (so I thought). Took my thoughts and pushed them aside. Things happened that left me no choice but to put me on paper and write. Judge not until you can face where you have been, and be able to look at you, with a much clearer picture of who you are, what you have done and who you're really not.

Thinking

Thinking got me in a mess a whole lot of times.

I thought this, I thought that. I thought right and wrong.

I thought I knew about love. Thought I was a good parent.

Thought my heart couldn't take no more.

I'm tired of this life.

I got to thinking of some awful things that just wasn't right.

I was fed up. Angry. Felt betrayed.

Lost things that weren't mine.

So, I got to thinking….and the thought felt good, because the only one in my thoughts was me.

I Gave Him Knowledge

I gave him knowledge, he didn't understand. By his gender, and society he believed he was the man, head of the house; the one to provide; father; dad; king of the castle; just some lies. *I gave him knowledge*; after all I came from his rib. I'm the one who knows the rhythm of his heart, the breaths he takes. The way to his heart is by the food I make. *I gave him knowledge* of how to take his time and make love. *I gave him knowledge* when he betrayed my trust; selfish me thought I taught him too much. *I gave him knowledge* of how a woman stands by her man. *I gave him knowledge* he just went too far. This last bit of knowledge, I left him with… Do you know I made you, raised you, loved you…now it's time to let go.

Picture Frame of Life

I put the pictures in a frame, walked past them and smiled at the *picture frame of life*. Many pictures different poses, mom and the kids. Oh so many pictures. Had a vacant spot. Not by my choosing, just a conscious decision that was made. *Picture frame of life* showed years of my life, without the picture frame being the *pictured frame of life*.

Children of a Seasoned Package

I watched my children from an infant. Along the way, I did some things wrong. Became a victim, developed into a volunteer of things I hadn't become. I watched them grow with me through pain, hurt, and struggles. Along the way I got lost, the season of time had me bound. I was the *season* of a package ripped apart, not just opened. *Children of a seasoned package* came from a package that still needed unwrapped.

Dust to Discovery

I came from the dust, well not exactly.

From the rib of the dust, I was formed.

Deceived by the enemy early destined my life's course.

Known the wrongs of actions placed upon me a huge loss.

No flesh of another human can take away my blame.

Form the *dust to discovery* is when I called Jesus' Name.

Cries Lost in a Crowd

I hear *cries lost in a crowd*, of such a busy place,

People moving, babies growing and changing faces.

I hear *cries lost in a crowd*, people living people dying.

Choices made to misbehave leaving tears on pillows.

I hear *cries lost in a crowd*, something happened.

The cries are so much nearer.

I hear *cries lost in a crowd* of the person I saw in the mirror.

I'm A Revised Edition

I'm a revised edition; you know how you do things then start over…

A *revised edition* has been made, looked over for mistakes and improvements.

A *revised edition* brings more than it had before.

A *revised edition* acknowledges the people who helped in the revision of something made better.

I'm a revised edition. I've been made, read, dropped, picked-up, and read cover to cover.

I'm a revised edition starting at the beginning.

Bowed Down to Peace

I stood up for chaos, struggles, and disagreements. I stood fighting for things that had no purpose or reason. I stood entangled in a world deceitful and destructive. I stood (though I laid down) for love on my back only to realize I really stood alone. I'm *bowed down to peace*. My knees are just too weak. I can't stand no longer. I'm *bowed down to peace* to again stand stronger.

When I Let Go

I held on from a child the tears and sorrows. I held on for protection, didn't make me stronger. I held on through the times when I didn't let go. I held on, learning about me, letting go when I thought I found me. I held on to the tales told to me, later the stones molded me. I held on, felt like I was sinking, drowning without a life jacket. I held on, no matter what was happening. I was determined to save my life. I held on and was set free *when I let go*.

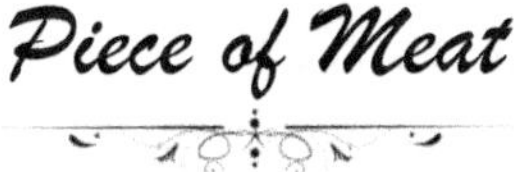

Piece of Meat

By the womb a *piece of meat* of a promise you were after. Somewhere along the way you changed plans, and what were you after. You began to need more than I, your manhood was sprung. Gave you a myth of how your world should be run. So, you came up with a plan and for a while it went undiscovered. You thought you were smooth and cocky. Betrayed friends didn't bother you the damage is done. You moved on. No big surprise. You left things along the way that cried for your attention. I still was there and gave my body to you. You left in me a chance of hope of us still being together. Those times ran out, and now we three are left alone. And in spite of it all I gave; found out you started another home. Broken down, torn apart. I thought I gave you the best part. But now I see what you gave me was just *a piece of meat.*

Affirmation of Truth

I'm an *affirmation of truth*.

I'm a woman to be discovered.

I'm built from a rib, that covered your breath.

I'm strong and mighty. I carry life in my body.

I'm built to last no matter how much I struggle.

I've been loved, abused, dazed, and confused.

I'm the source of your life, my place can't be denied.

Just look through the history of women before me, they brought the *affirmation of truth*.

Cry Out

I entered the world, with a *cry out.*

I fell down on the playground, with a *cry out.*

Didn't know I entered womanhood, with a *cry out.*

I had love plans end in a *cry out.*

I heard life through my body, *cry out.*

I was alone in my mind, I cried out.

Now I'm all cried out, the tears dried up.

My *cry out* now are cries of joy.

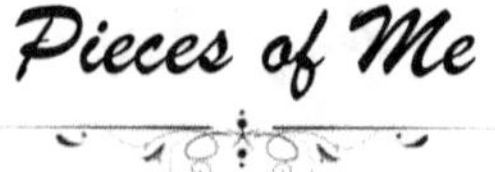

I never knew how many pieces held me together. The pieces of life put together like a puzzle. A little at a time, started with an outline reaching for pieces that would stick together. *Pieces of me* I picked up just didn't fit; used others hands for a different spot. *Pieces of me* I had to eventually start over. I was the only one who had the *pieces of me* that could finish the puzzle.

Struggle of A Mother

I'm the *struggle of a mother* for a lack of what I had. I'm the *struggle of a mother* as I struggle to care for what he left and all I had to care for. I'm the *struggle of a mother* watching faces look like I felt. I'm the *struggle of a mother* providing much more that what I had. I'm the *struggle of a mother* as I fight to protect and save gifts from my past. I'm the *struggle of a mother* made mistakes with many men and lost some dreams. I'm the *struggle of a mother*. I'm a mother whose soul survived being a motherless child.

Through the Fire

I walked *through the fire*. It was life as some called it. Passed the burns of my childhood and the char of my younger year's behaviors. I walked *through the fire*, getting burned by things I touched; doctored up the blisters, changed some habits. Now I walk with fire. The fire is through my soul.

Self-Inflicted

Self-inflicted things I suffered, through a journey called life. Loss of love, loss of self, and loss of my own life. Not death. Let me explain. *Self-inflicted* became a habit. *Self-inflicted* became a way when the pain didn't fit. I bargained myself away, for lustful visits to take away what was aching down in my pit. *Self-inflected* stopped working, when there were no feelings or pain I could blame.

Body Tight. Flesh Loose.

I was young. *Body tight.* Got my own thoughts. *Flesh loose. Body tight* did me right. Even if only for one night. *Flesh loose* brought me things; I gave them all middle names. *Body tight* became too loose; had my mind all confused. *Flesh loose* became a bore; couldn't take it anymore. *Body tight flesh loose* was longer an excuse. So, I tightened up the flesh. My mind and soul fit me best.

Taken In to Give Out

Born with a spirit to receive, tainted by a world that betrayed me. *Taken in* some things taught, others learned, most I bought. *Taken in* by man's deceitfulness of empty broken promises. *Taken in to give out*, bitterness claimed my soul. *Taken in to give out*, taken in my Father's love, to be given my place in my Father's Kingdom.

Carried Bitterness of Pain

I've *carried the bitterness of pain*; it was bought by broken dreams. Promised things of fulfillment, of love, family, prosperity, in a world broken. It's like a travel through time in what man built to take a trip to the moon. Carried through to another time and place where me never knew you. *Carried bitterness of pain* I now carry love and surrender to a life I thought I lost long ago.

Painted You

Painted you, painted me what did you see? As you painted your expectations, desires, and obligations on me, to a need you couldn't reach. Thought I could help you paint a better picture of me that you couldn't see. *Painted you* painted me, your past lost love that touched me with hands when I forgot. *Painted you* painted me in a time when I also forgot that I could change the painted picture you had of me.

Chained from Fear

Lost memories chained from fear of rejection and lost hope. Chained from fear the childhood that was once took. All the decisions made for my life, chained from the fear of being alone. Chained from fear always took me, in my mind to a place that kept me safe. My mind played a trick and kept me chained to fear instead. Chained from fear now I know was the chain that kept me bound so I couldn't be found.

Victim and Assailant

I'm a victim of me, have been an assailant of my life. I' an assailant of what my heart desires, a victim who lost a cause. I'm a victim with courage, standing up for the fight. I'm an assailant losing a battle, the victim has started to fight back. I'm not a victim to my assailant. I fought and won. I got my life back.

Yielding

Yielding from a place that was comfortable and ignorant. Believing what was happening, was all the things my life could handle. *Yielding* into a cautious place where I always was the driver. Belief of control will cause a crash, an explosion in your soul. *Yielding* to finally come to a place, where the window of life becomes clear.

Past Paid For

Past paid for the thoughts of a broken child. *Past paid* for young love lost in webs of lies. *Past paid* for in the lessons of becoming a mother. *Past paid* for in a single parent home structure. *Past paid* for tangled in a webbed disease of self-destruction. *Past paid* for risen I rise. *Past paid* for my past I survived.

Who is She?

Who is she? As I look in the mirror. Change clothes, hair, her face remains familiar. Built up confidence don't hide the disaster of where you've been, what you've done, nor numerous encounters. Lustful, unfulfilling decisions of disaster; the old song with drinks that had you thinking you were invincible. Took your ass on a ride; it was fun while it lasted. Chased something never ending; got lost in the dust when the smoke was clear from the rubble; your driving seemed to have stopped. Your vision seems clear, you decide to proceed with caution. Start over your journey with new eyes perfect vision. New mirror of the face that smiled back at you, asking *who is she?*

Wanted

Wanted to be loved, looked the wrong way.

Wanted to be liked, to take away the pain.

Wanted to be understood, never happened.

Wanted to be committed, wasn't what they were after.

Wanted to be a mother, reached by hindsight.

Wanted to be courageous, to stand and fight.

Wanted to be victorious, in spite of my decisions.

Wanted to be accomplished, with a finished vision.

Wanted to be a lot of things, most didn't happen.

Wanted to be, I became **Moné Parker.**

Circumstances of Thinking

Circumstances of thinking caught me, in a web of lies. *Circumstances of thinking* taught me my will to survive. In my darkest hour when I stood back against the wall. And everyone who I thought was there had left; there I stood alone. *Circumstances of thinking* caught me by surprise. *Circumstances of thinking* is the last thought. My thoughts are no longer my circumstances.

Battery Operated

Let me begin this story. Girl take a seat and grab a cup of coffee. It's a little tale about a *battery-operated* fairytale. It started not long ago because I was used to skin. Somewhere along this path to self, C battery became my friend. I had stocked my dresser up. We met many nights. Some long. Some short. Some sweaty. I have to admit, some just a bore. It took some time to figure out how to make the batteries last long. Then one night, just by chance. I joined in to play along. I had the music low. Gerald Levert was playing for a while. Then Jodeci started singing *Freakin' You.* I pictured his face. Didn't realize, but it was a surprise *battery-operated.* Got lost. There was no mirror to see my face....but my toes curled...my body trembled. I just kept it there to take me back, as Luther would say… "If Only for One Night." I tell you no lie; it wasn't a surprise *battery-operated* and I laid fast asleep.

Consequences

Consequences of my circumstance, by now I made some decisions. Let me start by sharing what we will call "it". To tell the truth, *consequences* of situations made by vacant thoughts. Mind made decisions; very few ever fought. Listen, I tell you no lies. I need to speak the truth of how my *consequences* became the root of my success. Put me in a place where I had to ponder my mistakes. Look at my life. Rethink my choices. *Consequences* won't be the end of my story.

Designed and Structured Different

I'm *designed and structured different*. Beautifully and wonderfully made. My hair, my eyes, my nose, my lips. My whole body designed to pull me through the worst of pain. Structured to birth children. Who else you know is designed and structured to help build-up a man? I've been born. I've been torn. I've' been beat. I've been left. I've been called other things than my name. Yet through it all, I stand for my cause; I won't be defeated. I was *designed and structured different*.

Unfamiliar Territory

I have been to a place never visited before. You know the odd thing? I could only enter through the back door. I had no clear view. It was always cloudy or maybe smoke filled the rooms. I saw several doors. None had an exit sign. As I reached for the handle, the door stood still. One after another. This can't be real. Suddenly moments of life flashed before me. I ran down the hall. The last door that I tried took me out of this *unfamiliar territory*.

Punished People

I ran with *punished people*. We ran far and long. Uphill. Downhill. Even marathons. I couldn't even consider the lessons each one taught. You know you never realized the theme played a favorite song. Lyrics of *punished people* played on themselves. You didn't know you was invited. They didn't know you brought them along. It was the words of the last lyrics that *punished people*. Let go of the punishment inflicted on self.

A Matter of Convenience

Let me talk about it girl! I just couldn't believe it! I have to start with how it became a *matter of convenience*. It was one of those days, I was feeling right. Hair done. Nails done. Clothes just right. I wasn't looking for no booty call. I just didn't have the time. He walked in. Edged up. Sharp. Jeans, flannel and some Timbs. Although really not my type. Eyes crossed paths. It became too much. I moved in; he came close. Barely speaking a word. We each knew the thoughts were there. The night would end. We knew later it was a *matter of convenience*.

Just Risen

It came up one morning.

My eyes met the glare of the sun.

This time, unlike many other days, I didn't squint or blink.

My eyes laid upon a full bright sunshine.

Didn't realize how long I stood gazin' at the sun.

The warmth soothed me.

Felt like a just right shower after a good night's sleep.

You know how it gets you ready for the day.

It started to go down, almost move away slow.

I hadn't felt like this in a while.

As I turned away my soul spoke to me with just these words.

The voice said *"just risen"!!!*

Yesterday

Yesterday I had a talk with my body and soul. At first it mumbled. I couldn't understand it. I settled down in a deeper thought so I could comprehend. It started in my mind with thoughts I had of how things had become. I started to shake my head; the thoughts were too much. Tears rolled down my face. I couldn't breathe. I started to pant. I had to relax. My soul began to feel at ease. *Yesterday* I knew something had changed. *Yesterday* I was released from me.

Soul at War with My Body

It wasn't a fist fight, the OK corral, gang wars or senseless crimes. It was a one-woman battle for full rights of things lost long ago. It started innocent, playing hide-n-seek. It progressed with age and time. The stories got deeper. The pain unbearable. It felt like my body began to seep. Everything was flooding out. My mind ran the race to catch up. I couldn't ignore the signs of distress. It had taken its toll. I got down on my knees. Prayed for God's armor for the *soul at war with my body*.

Saved

Shh…I hear the sounds. Cries of pain. Low self-esteem. Lost love and mistakes all paid by visions awakened. Check the heart. It tells no lies. Through it the tongue speaks the truth, buried inside full of pride. Body entangled, just a mess. For protection to make corrections of the soul; bound indiscretions that hindered my life lessons to become a true woman of God. Now I know my past is paid for. Jesus paid for it on the cross.

Smiling Faces

I smile. You smile. We smile. What does the smile mean? Can you see behind the smile? The frown behind those cheeks. Smiles tell lies, portraying just a façade of things kept buried. Burdens heavy and damage deeply rooted. The smile represents a face of feelings that each day shows a different broken window. A different life told, just a rainbow of colored deceit.

Good Vibrations

I remember floating on *good vibrations* thinking life was fun. My life, I thought, had just begun. The freedom, the adventure, the simplest of things all taken for granted. Famous words spoken…"I'm grown. You can't tell me what to do!" became a broken record in my head. What I forgot is things don't last. There is no end to a rainbow. *Good vibrations* came to an end. Now the famous words came into play, here it goes…"See, I told your grown ass!" That *good vibrations* don't mean a thing.

# Say Yes

You don't always *say yes*, yet this is the flesh fed for desires forbidden; selfish decisions; spiteful consequences; and lust. No doesn't seem feasible when you feel like your pleasure has been violated. You get what you want 99.9% of the time. *Say Yes.* I played this game for far too long. You taught me how to maneuver those things that couldn't tell you no, so that's what I used. It kept you confused. Just enough to *say yes.*

Again Tomorrow

No, not *again tomorrow*. I won't put myself in a mess. I played this charade, and never guessed, I felt it a waste of time. Yesterday came and I couldn't figure out why I did some things over again thinking it was something. I wanted from the other day, knowing I was playing repeat on myself. I wasn't clueless. The way we played became useless. I made up my mind that, *again tomorrow*, I would do me different.

Awakened Annoyed

I fell asleep easy like any other night. Had hot tea and a cigarette, said my prayers; turned off the light. I could feel my body toss and turn. Was I dreaming or just uncomfortable? I thought maybe one thought would soothe my mind and make me sleep. He came from way long ago, someone, something, some feeling, that once made me smile. I proceeded to encounter. I could feel the smile on my face. Then my body lay at rest. The thing of that mind set lingered to the morning. I rose *awakened annoyed.*

Boundaries of Self-Protection

I was wild and free. Yes, I had boundaries. You know of the things and how far I would go. Met many people who wanted different things. Some too much for the asking. The ones I indulged didn't turn out to be real love. I felt disappointed. I became a creature of seducing to assure I was satisfied. Yet as time passed, my desires began to change. I was there. I needed something more than given. So, I made a choice. It set up the course for *boundaries of self-protection*.

Delayed Gratification

I began it a long time ago. See, early on, I gave my body for instant satisfaction. I didn't pay no attention because I couldn't slow down. My experience was "I have to get mine before you get yours." Anyway, that's probably all your after. Time went on; the satisfaction was gone and no longer soothed my sexual appetite. I took a piece of paper, wrote just a few names. That was really all it took. I sat back, had some thoughts and a laugh. Smoked a cigarette. Blinded from the smoke, realized how I had been having *delayed gratification.*

Instant Match

You ever play the game where you put the cards down then turn them one by one to make a match? You ever notice how long it takes to get them all right. I led you to how this will end. Dark skin, light bright, just like the shade of caramel, even Caucasian. Brown eyes, light brown eyes, hazel and blue. Blue jeans, Dickies, sweats, dress slacks. Sometimes even a tie. Public transportation, rental car, baby momma car or jitney. Hustling. No job. Living with mommy. Asking you see where I'm going. I'm just showing off what it takes you through for an *instant match*.

Last Time You Loved Me

We had been through all the things that end a relationship. Yet I still cared. We both played a part, no single blame. Still friends we promised each other. Sometimes I would see you and want to be with you. You were with a friend, no disrespect. I'm better than that. It was a summer day. Months later I seen you. The sun was shining. I remembered the times you were mine. You were alone. I approached and asked, could this be the *last time you loved me?*

Insatiable Taste

I'm gonna take you some place that has a required taste. I hope your taste buds are ready. Let's begin by stating facts. This taste is very unique. Before you indulge, you need to know your taste for things will never be the same. I was ready for love and inexperienced, yet we took our time. This may sound weak, but yes, we played slow music to unwind. We kissed and caressed. We peeled away layers slowly to the beat of the music. After a while we lay skin to skin. He licked me smoothly just to soothe me; parts of my body tingled. I kind of got nervous. Thoughts filled my head of what it was like. How could I behave and give something away only for my husband? Emotions were high. The passion was so exhilarating. Before I knew it, it was done. Oh damn. Didn't know how to feel this can't be real. It was such an *insatiable taste*. I liked it.

MMM...MMM...Good

I heard *mmm...mmm...good.* I needed to know how *mmm...mmm...good* felt. Let's go on a journey. Maybe a cruise of how my body went through *mmm...mmm...good.* I was young. I got that feeling. I wanted, got relieved, so I thought mmm...was good. Yet I still changed my mind about what I was getting. I needed a different feeling. Let's start the cruise now. We gonna dock at different ports. Visit places around the world. May stay too long in cities and come back to familiar territory. I need to say the beginning turned me loose. Showed me things, bells rang. I was testing the waters out. I thought I became experienced. It became a bore. I had to move on. The student became the teacher. Wait. Let me explain this student part. I was young, I thought I had to use things. I was taught and those I learned from being a "good" student. *mmm...mmm...good* took me through, maybe what I was after. Yet my trip wasn't complete. *mmm...mmm...good* let me know I couldn't grow into the woman I wanted to be, *if mmm....mmm...good* was all I knew.

Taste Me

I was ready and thought of only one thing, but then I was shown. I felt his lips touch my love. I almost jumped back. I didn't know what to do. Slowly I felt the rush of my love come down. It was different. Felt great, let me say spectacular. The sensation through my body. Girl…. let me tell you! My heart skipped a beat while he made a moaning sound. Then I heard words as he talked to my love with the stroke of his tongue. My body went weak. He continued on. The he did something. Now I know what it was. His tongue played the drums, his fingers stroked the keys. While he played his song to *taste me*.

Working Arrangement

Through our decisions to make provisions of what we thought we had. We didn't really try to complete and find out what we did wrong. At best we became better friends than lovers. We talked about everything. Later we would find, through long conversations, not blame; just acceptance of the part we both played. We became best friends. Other couldn't see. Yet they tried to define what we had. It didn't matter, we didn't have a marriage. Our relationship was the best because we had a *working arrangement.*

One Little Choice

One little choice changed my life. Sat me down. Yet didn't make me your wife. So, what now? The choice I made, laid a plan in mind. Only your plan wasn't what I planned. My mind became confused. Time went on. I watched my family grow; yes, we multiplied, since the plan I made wasn't part of life's plan. I had to make up in my mind, to move on. It wasn't over just because of one too many choices.

Grandma Told Me

You heard that saying, "*grandma told me* there would be days like this." Doesn't touch on the surface of the things that I missed. I wasn't paying attention. She would say "I became hot in the ass." Not exactly. I had already given my ass away because I thought I earned it. *Grandma told me* some things that still are with me today, like food, clothing and shelter, keep money on hand just in case of an emergency. Grandma, I guess, loved me in her own special way. That was all she had. Through it all, now I realize, I should have paid more attention to the lessons *grandma told me*.

Remembered Places

I got some shit with me, sometimes. I got to laugh at myself. Look here. I went through my mind and brought along my body. Sometimes the real thing is not needed. And after reading, you'll understand how *remembered places* was safest. Been there. Done that. Could go skin if I wanted to, but sometimes I didn't want to see faces. So, I made a list. Sunday through Saturday. Placed names in my schedule where they would fit. The mental picture played, especially on the weekend, where those mmm…mmm…good ones should be. All the rest placed after a hard day's work. Baby…Times filled my head, *remembered places* were in bed. Sometimes part way through I had to change. The scheduled place wasn't too much to be remembered. All in all, I had a ball. You have to make *remembered places* for all the time you may have wasted in trying to keep *remembered places* real.

Looking For Daddy

Little girls, they say, grow up looking for someone like their daddy. I beg to differ sometimes, even sleeping children know silent things. Today is much different. Single mom family home is the family picture. *Looking for daddy* becomes meeting your brother or your sister, not a shame but just the same. Some don't mind if you call someone else daddy. I wouldn't blame it on society, or he's doing what his father did. That would be easy. See, the realness of things can't be old clichés, because reality paints a bigger picture for children today. You're better off not even bothering. Stick with MAMA. Stay *looking for daddy*.

The Main Part

My story has many things that make up the whole book. There is an introduction of who I am. Let's not forget the perfect title. There are the contents of what you will be entitled to read. There is the conclusion, let's just say really the beginning. There will be notes about the author, with such a beautiful cover. The gift I bring in writing me is that you don't forget or miss the *main part*.

Sequels to Love

I would be the first to say *sequels to love* aren't always needed. I've tried them with no avail, realizing I was just torturing myself. The feelings the first time gave, wasn't love so I erased it. Silly me kept looking for repeat performances, hoping this time it was a different time, different reason, different season, didn't matter. So now I learned sequels have an ending especially when love doesn't enter from the beginning.

Move On

I'm giving what I got, because I allowed it to happen, after we played back-up partners for instant satisfaction. Things I knew; I wasn't the only one. It was so damn good. I kept it for you despite all I knew because you came back so often. This one particular night the orgasms didn't seem right. You had made this peculiar sound, more than once. I listened closely. I never got confused. You called me, not my name. The feeling went dry. That's when I knew I had to *move on*.

Stay Still

Stay still. Let me teach you. I been dying to meet you. We played eye contact where we totally undressed each other. *Stay still*. I wanna show you how my body was made for you. Just *stay still* and relax. *Stay still*. Let me control you; let me push the buttons; only forward will be used. This is my movie debut made just for you. You. No cameras to record. Play close attention. *Stay still* and watch while I play me for you.

Can't Stop

You ever taste something so good you just *can't stop* eating.

You just want more and more til' you're full.

That was the feelings I got.

I can't begin to tell you why.

I knew better, but something had me, it had all of me.

Not just my body.

I mean…this thing didn't betray me.

It was actually the opposite faithful to no ends.

I wondered where did I find it, how to keep it.

I'm gonna have to fight to keep what's mine.

I don't wanna let go.

I just don't know how.

I'm really stuck for this taste, I *can't stop.*

Lost Identity

Somewhere, somehow through something I lost pieces of me. Had to do some searching for my identity. Things had happened it's called life, it's just I didn't know. I would almost lose me in the process. The pain. The tears. The questions of my actions and behaviors that inflicted my soul; feelings that lingered long and had my body weak. I didn't know me sometimes. I had to look real hard in the mirror. I didn't like who looked back. She was unfamiliar. That look scared me. I realized I had lost my identity. And I knew I wanted me back.

In the Midst of a Mess

I been bound by things I did to myself.

Holding me accountable for making a mess.

Bound by an entity that disrupted my destiny.

Collisions enclosed my desires.

Decisions halted my dreams.

I been put down to be brought up.

I cried for other things than myself.

I kept laughter as my medicine, it was my soul sensation.

It was supposed to medicate my brokenness.

I tried a lot of things *in the midst of my mess.*

Then I discovered Jesus was in the *midst of the mess,* just waiting patiently with me.

The Morning After

It was in *the morning after*. I remembered, yet wanted to forget, how I stood as a silhouette, looking at me MC Repeat. Things that really had no end. It was the same thing just a different face. Not every day just some meantime endings. Some "oh I thought of you again…it feels good…what time? How about 8?" *The morning after* wasn't even really meaningful while it lasted. Thing is I never wanted morning to come with your face still on my pillow, even though our bodies met in agreement. The effect was gone. Now let's move on. I got a morning after of being alone.

Masks

They hide you. You place them to cover what's hidden. Where only eyes are seen, which is said to be windows to the soul. How many masks hide what your body has captured? Could your body change with the masks you paraded through the pain you allowed and collected? Masks take away strength of a soul searching for freedom. Masks do come off.

After the Bar

Back then, after the bar was the after party. It was him and my body. How could I be there. I was tasted, roasted and fully cooked. Yet I did remember the things that my body proclaimed in his name. Because all the fluid that entered my body came through my pores, then my body moved like a ballerina. He was swift. Graceful. And performed exceptionally well. This is our secret. I couldn't resist. He was my *after the bar* hangover.

Pictures of Me

Look, what I done. I placed *pictures of me* across the table. I was amazed at what I saw. It was different faces, stages, poses, clothes and sometimes, other people. I looked at them closely and realized sometimes it didn't look like me. I analyzed my face, remembered the times, laughed, and also cried. *Pictures of me* told a story. They say pictures are worth a thousand words. That day I started my story. *Pictures of me* I can't let fade.

Turned Out

Wow! What a way to lose. Things done for selfish reasons. Not always the most pleasing results. I'm talking from experience, just a friendly conversation of a situation that has no end. I wanted it. I got it. I had it. As long as I wanted it. No matter when or what time of day, it didn't matter. I was ready. My body was on beat. The rhythm steady. Yes, he was my jones. One day it hit me. I didn't get it. Hadn't had for about a week. I thought this is crazy. My body is craving. *I'm turned out* and done lost my rhythm.

Filled Appetite

I was full. Couldn't eat. I didn't know I had been fed a full course meal that laid my body to sleep. I had chocolate as the main dish, nothing else needed; my sweet tooth was fed. I divulged with sweet delight. Every inch of my body was satisfied from my head to my feet. I tell you this, with all that my body felt my appetite was filled.

Chocolate does my body the best.

You Were Someone Else

If I told you lies, would you feel at ease because of the games life played? I been there a few too many times. It's no fun when everything you see, feel, and believe isn't true. So, through this I've learned, even though it might hurt you often without incident, or harm, that you were someone else. They weren't there. You fit the criteria of what I felt at the moment. Don't get me wrong. We both played along. You just never knew, now you do, that you were *someone else*.

Body Made for Man

My body, not what the world sees it should be, but the wonderfully made beauty is me. Taken for granted for selfish things. Given too easy with nothing gained. I thought my *body was made for man.* I gave, I gave all that I had. My body made beats to the sound of his voice. My body for him gave me no choice on how to behave. My body didn't ask my permission. He claimed full rights to how my body moved. With every position he played my body. I fully gave because my *body was made for man.* My body made me a slave to him.

I Forgot Me

I forgot me, lost what I hadn't looked to find. Put so much in other things. Men, running…just because things seemed out of place. Yeah, I was there. Was it my mind? Most of the time just my body. I forgot to feel how to be real with the things that entered my world. *I forgot me* and cast aside any chance of happiness. I didn't want to even get caught by feelings, lust or lies. So, I forgot to remind myself not to forget to love myself by the things I forgot about me.

Feeling Like I Been Got

Oh no! This ain't and can't happen. My body trying to control my mind by the things it's getting. It's trying to tell me: "don't you like how you feel? It's what you've been missing." I like it. I want it. It's been the best so far yet. It makes us as one. We move in beat, and we are oh so happy. Remember how you was talking about you think you lost your grove? Well…listen to me. This feeling doesn't have to stop. My body had my mind *feeling like I had been got.*

Unfulfilled Need

I thought I could be okay with the justs, the sometimes, the in between times and the not reallys. False fabrications of needs, only claimed by an empty body. Maybe it was the liquor, the weed, cocaine, or crack. Leaving traces of unfulfillment. Emptying my soul, only left me just a shell of a vessel, searching for an *unfulfilled need* that would never fill the *unfulfilled need* that lay bound by needy decisions.

Right Purpose

If two wrongs don't make a right, I've been calling this personal thing, my right purpose to find what's left right inside of me. Not a dilemma, just a situation on making right some purpose of the life. I made decisions and caused anything that may have not been right to have no purpose at all. I'm not justifying or rationalizing, just my perspective wasn't for purpose, just made-up rights of my own. Didn't do me no good. No. Not at all. Even when rights never felt wrong. Just through it all, now I know those wrongs happened for the *right purpose.*

Wrong Place, Wrong Time

What the fuck is going on? I come when I'm asked. I'm at the wrong place. Could there be something I missed? R. Kelly's lyrics saying: *"your body's telling me yes, but my mind's telling me no."* *Wrong place, wrong time.* Done lost my right place of where I'm used to being. I don't remember natures call like this. *"In my mind I'll always be his lady."*

Wrong place, wrong time. Trying to change my *"sexual healings."* Oh no stop! *Wrong place, wrong time.* Won't be a time I'll have to choose to forget what went wrong, and a time among some others I hide to forget.

Causing Something to Cause Something

I've done many things. Caused something that was really nothing. My self-seeking. Tired of that. What I thought of you really didn't matter. I *was causing something to cause something,* with no strings attached. It was my history that had integrated me; my masculinity side was in full bloom. I did me. Passed you as if we hadn't met. Sometimes my mind would play you again. I was *causing something to cause something* when I didn't want to be bothered with causing something again.

The Quiet Storm

The storm of my life came towering in ripping apart pieces of my life. The storm started slow. How could I have known the damage it would leave in its path. I need to say there were times when I sensed signs of danger. Always saying to myself the storm will pass, and it did. Just for a short while. This, I realize now, was the big storm with no sign of letting up. I braced, took cover, prayed, and discovered that after it was over. I was in the *quiet storm* of life.

First Love Tears

I shed many tears of ha-ha first love. At least that's what I thought. My knowledge grew and what I discovered is those tears were made of something I needed to go through. Damn it was painful. The tears arranged from one-night stands, months, some years, and things I've done to myself. When the Kleenex box and half the roll was gone, I blew my nose, wiped the lost tear away and promised myself to have no more *first love tears* because the first love would be myself.

Emptied Out

I heard my soul cry, my heart ache, numbness in my spirit. I see the thoughts of my mind play "this is your life" rewinding back the hands of time. Just glimpses and pieces. Seasons and reasons, things done in the name of love. Many faces. Very few places. Just situations that kept me filled up disguised as things called life. All of a sudden, the tape moved forward. The view was different. I took a deep breath, shook my head. Knew this was it. I've been *emptied out* for a better chance at life.

Meantime Love

It took a while for me to discover the way love works. The ups and downs the ins and outs. The *meantime love* of what I went through. It's sad to say I always thought that old meantime was the best. Yet meanwhile, I waited and sometimes debated if I wanted it back to feed my *meantime love* with false hope. Deceiving myself. I didn't want that feeling of being lonely. The *meantime love* stopped coming through the feeling of what was gone. Now I'm in my own *meantime love* getting back on track.

I Forgive You, For Me

I cried many nights. For me, wondering why did my soul weep. I didn't talk to anyone but me to explain it. I looked at me as the source of the pain. Taking blame doesn't always explain why. When it's over you can't see clearer. Let me explain. I wanted you for some odd reason to be my reason for doing things right. My just because wasn't even enough. After my blaming was through that's when I knew, *I forgive you, for me.*

Changed Me, For You

Damn, here I go again playing changing faces. The everything about me, believing the light that went out was about you. I'm not saying I've played with changes one too many times. I've just seen through my history that things changed in my mirror that faced me. I thought it was me. Silly rabbit. The changes so you would or could not be distracted from what I was giving. It wasn't enough. I betrayed my own trust. Now I'm wondering why did I believe *changed me, for you* existed.

Rebound

Like a ball, the world keeps bouncing. I had the hands that keep the rhythm of the ball in beat. Making choices without thinking, letting feelings speed up the beat of the sound the ball was making. I made jump shots for love. Had two pointers all the time. Tried layups that were missed. I never hit three's from outside the line. A couple times I fouled out. Playing the game became almost second nature, until I realized, all you seem to get is a *rebound*.

Who Is He?

I had been looking for what they call Mr. Right. I didn't go on the Internet or revisit familiar faces, which was a waste of time. Been there. Done that. I wanted to be loved. Didn't want a wet ass. I'm too old for booty calls. I felt it was time to get serious about the things he should offer. Be 100% in himself, have goals, not hoes; a baby mama with some class; ain't playing no games; has a job and a car. Now I'm led to wonder, just *who is he* or if he exists?

Suited in Brown

Something happened. Changed my life. It was in the blink of an eye. Now I'm sitting trying to focus behind the walls of the gate *suited in brown*. What a color to be dressed in for some days of your life. Everywhere you look you see D.O.C. labels on backs. Let me get you to a place of how I get through and some things I seen, *suited in brown*. My outside world wasn't clueless, yet this scene is new to me. Sometimes it seems I'm not far from home, but wait a minute; I've seen things, new to me. Check it out. Pot in a bucket; homemade real dishes in a bag; artists at work making masterpieces; fights; arguments; and a woman changing their souls wanting to be men. Not much to be offered, more of a sit down to realize where you went wrong. Women coming. Women going. Coming back with new numbers. What does it mean? I violated. You can hear it all bounce off the walls of the chit-chatter. Cries of lost souls. I tell you no lie, it seems this is a different world. All you hear are cries for help. Maybe in time the little girls will realize they can change the color being *suited in brown*.

A Cracked Place

I'm gonna take you back for a minute. It deals with feelings and emotional baggage of childhood scars, emotional losses, abuse and betrayal of love. Childhood scars of separation. I lost my mother young. Didn't really hit without the memories of being a motherless child. Emotional losses became the cost of looking for love in all the wrong places. Then came the abuse of what I discovered was laid internally by their past. It was the betrayal of love that brought me to the *cracked places* in my soul.

Unforgettable

It's been a long time. Sometimes I reminiscence about the things I deemed *unforgettable*. Silly of me to look at things that passed through my soul. I thought it was *unforgettable* how he was the 1st one and the different stages of love that he took me through. *Unforgettable* was the things I felt, first made of something called sex. Then his hands betrayed me so I wouldn't forget and left a mark on my heart. Now *unforgettable* is the meaning of what no other man will be to me.

About the Author

Moné Parker was born in Brooklyn, New York and now resides in Pennsylvania. She is the mother of five children and eleven grandchildren. Sacred Notes is the first book of many books of her experiences with loneliness, grief, pain, and finding the love that kept her from herself. While reading these poems, allow yourself to be open to the burdens of your soul. Her hope is through reading this book it opens the freedom to a peace that she learned she can share with others. Hopefully these expressions of words will allow you to see that you can have peace.

www.ingramcontent.com/pod-product-compliance
Lightning Source LLC
Chambersburg PA
CBHW051828150726
47998CB00001B/338